# The Beautiful Change

## By

## Armando Perez

Cover Artwork // Vladimir Fedoltov and Tom Barrett

"The Love of Jesus Christ is the only motive that will sustain you. Every circumstance, every issue, every heart ache, every sin, and every evil, shall bow before King Jesus!"

- Armando Perez

# The Whosoevers

I used to think I had to be perfect. I spent most of my life trying to make others like me because I wanted to feel accepted by them. Many people have been told that popularity and money is the definition of success. But that is not what success looks like to God. Success as a believer is having a relationship with God and believing in Him.

**John 3:16 (KJV) For God so loved the world, that he gave his only begotten Son, that whosoever believeth in Him should not perish, but have everlasting life.**

Notice in the passage of John 3 it says, "that WHOSOEVER believes!"

It doesn't say "only an elect few who figure out how to have a perfect life and then choose to believe."

God isn't expecting you to achieve perfection without Him. Apart from His help it is impossible to even come close. The truth is we all need Him.

DON'T BELIEVE THE LIE that if you mess up or fail God will never forgive you.

Jesus: the son of God gave HIS life for YOU. He was and is perfect, and His sacrifice saved us from our past and present failures.

Be encouraged that no one is perfect! The blood of Jesus washes away the stains of your life. And the love of Jesus makes you perfectly acceptable.

# Saving Grace

The capacity of God's love is hard to try and figure out. Almost everyone has been taught to give love when they've received love. In other words, if someone treats you right and makes you feel good, then it's ok to love them.

Aren't you glad that we weren't saved by how good we had to become? Instead, our salvation was given because of how good God is. Even if you were the worst sinner that had ever lived, Jesus still chose to give up His life for you!

He knows more about you than anyone else on this planet. He sees deep into your heart, and He knows the value in each of us.

It doesn't matter what you've done or how far you feel that you could have run away from Him. He still loved you enough to die a sinner's death and redeem your life!

Life with God isn't the easy way out, but it's the only way.

Jesus said, "No one can come to the Father except through me". John 14:6

Not everyone will understand your journey... but that's ok. They aren't supposed to. God has a special purpose for your life, and it begins, remains, and will sustain in a personal relationship with Him.

Remember... no one is perfect.

**1 Peter 5:8 (ISV) Be clear-minded and alert. Your opponent, the devil, is prowling around like a roaring lion, looking for someone to devour.**

There will be times that it will not be easy to believe, but it's in those times that your greatest defense is to STILL BELIEVE!

When the opposition comes, remember that the same God, who saved you at your worst, is the same God that is still in your corner. He still loves, He still forgives, and He still saves!

It makes for a good church service or street outreach to preach the message of salvation something like this, "As a sinner you must give your life to Jesus to be saved." That's what most Christians have been taught. Even though it seems like the noblest of acts and it is true that we must surrender our old life, there is a much more powerful truth.

Jesus gave His life for you and if you receive it, He gives His life TO YOU!

And by His Grace alone - you have been given the answer to every circumstance in your life. All you must do is BELIEVE!

# In the Fire

## 2 Corinthians 12:9 (NLT) "My grace is all you need. My power works best in weakness."...

Through many years of teaching and outreach, I've seen the power and undeniable presence of God move in streets, schools, restaurants, and churches. As a Christian, it has become an adopted language to say, "I'm Blessed." And it's just as easy to tell someone, "Everything is going well", when the truth is there are challenges you are dealing with. Honestly, just because you made the decision to follow Jesus, it doesn't mean that you're always going to feel like every single day is a 'Holy and Glorious' moment.

We serve a Mighty God, and He is a God of miracles. He could surely take away all the bad of the world and physically change your circumstances, but there is something that is more important to Him than for your life to be painlessly perfect. That 'something' is that you become the man or woman that He created you to be.

In saying that, I mean that God is more interested in the progress of the process. He's more interested in your heart. He's more interested in the allowance of life's uncertainty, that through Faith, you will become STRONGER and BETTER than you ever thought possible.

We can easily look at a finished product in the natural and set goals to accomplish the things that we desire most, but when it comes to the invisible supernatural realm of our personal spiritual lives, we often find it much more difficult to accept that it takes time.

When you look back at the Garden of Eden, it was never God's plan to set humanity in a perfect environment. God knew that there would be snakes in that garden. In the same way, it's not always the plan that your life be perfect and free from circumstances. But it's God's ultimate plan that we learn to become an OVERCOMER in every situation!

"Look!" Nebuchadnezzar shouted. "I see four men, unbound, walking around in the fire unharmed! And the fourth looks like a god!" Daniel 3:25

(Full Story of the Blazing Furnace, Daniel 3)

In the story of the three Hebrew boys, notice that God didn't drown the flames with water. He didn't destroy the furnace and burn down the city that stood against them. No... God Himself showed up, and He stood in the fire WITH THEM! He guarded them... and He walked right beside them in that scorching perilous pit!

You see, living in an imperfect world is not a curse, but a blessing. It gives you the opportunity to be closely connected to God. He's allowed His Spirit to live inside of you, so that the wisdom - and knowledge - and power of His Glory could shine through you to the entire world!

Take a moment; to thank God for the Grace we've been given. It is more than enough for the challenges you may face. Pray for wisdom that will allow you to see, no matter what you face - HE IS WITH YOU!

Day 4

**You gain nothing by setting your eyes on the problem.
You gain everything by keeping your focus on Jesus.**

# Heart Change

I have seen many people who love God and who have been touched by the sacrifice of Jesus but have failed to see a transformation of their heart and renewal of their mind beyond their salvation.

I believe when David asked the Lord to "create in him a pure heart" (Psalm 51), He wasn't saying the 'Sinner's Prayer'. - He was telling God that he believed in Him, and that he needed to know Him in the deepest way possible.

I believe he was saying - "God, I need you. And I know that you are bigger than anything that this life could ever offer me. Show me YOUR ways and let me see your face. Help me to see life from YOUR perspective and let me know love the way you do. I acknowledge YOUR POWER - my life is weak and is NOTHING without your heart in me."

Fast forward to today, and our prayer language should sound less of "God, I NEED you" and more "God I RECIEVE you, through what YOUR SON paid the price for ME to have."

You can't transform your heart or renew your mind in your own personal strength and power.

It's the acknowledgment that the fulfillment of the old covenant and through the finished work completion of the cross, we have been given the FULL ETERNAL

CONNECTION of the New Covenant created by Jesus Christ! The moment you receive His life and the moment you receive His Spirit; you are redeemed and restored and placed in right standing with the Father.

Only in that truth can we ever see the human heart changed.

# <u>Prevailer</u>

You are NOT a disappointment to God!

You are Chosen by Him!

Appointed by Him!

Saved by Him!

Restored by Him!

Redeemed through Him!

Loved by Him!

Cleansed by Him!

Embraced by Him!

Sanctified by Him!

A New Creation through Him!

Empowered by Him!

And only by His STRENGTH and by His SPIRIT you will find Life!

**Romans 5:6-8 (NLT)**

**When we were utterly helpless, Christ came at just the right time and died for us sinners. Now, most people would not be willing to die for an upright person,**

**though someone might perhaps be willing to die for a person who is especially good. But God showed his great love for us by sending Christ to die for us while we were still sinners.**

He's not waiting for you to 'fix' the way you are - He died for you knowing who you are.

REPENT - TRUST Him - BELIEVE Him - and FOLLOW Him!

Hold on to His Promise for your life, believe that He loves you, and make the declaration that you will never give in to the lie that you are a disappointment.

# Deadweight

The blood of Jesus removes you from sin, the stain of sin, the sting of sin, the effects of sin, the reminder of sin, and the mark of sin.

But notice I said it removes YOU from sin. It's important to know that the action of Jesus' sacrifice removed sin's power over you, but it didn't remove sin from the earth.

**1 Peter 2:24 (NLT) He personally carried our sins in His body on the cross so that we can be dead to sin and live for what is right...**

By receiving the gift of salvation, we often mistake the idea that our new life will automatically become a life free from all sin and temptations, and that because we chose to follow God - He is supposed to magically take all the evil in the world away.

That idea can wear you down with a "works mentality" that says you must do everything in your own power to avoid sin, because sin is bad, and if you even think about sin, God will be displeased in you.

It is true that God despises sin, but the bible tells us Jesus died for our sins.

The scripture says, "He was made a curse for us as He took upon Himself ALL OUR SINS."

Remember this, "Grace saved you. And Grace will carry you!"

You didn't sign up to be an employee of Heaven to take on the job of trying to be Holy. Through Christ's sacrifice you've been given the mind of Christ and if you live with a righteous conscience, it will produce fruit to holiness without you trying to be Holy.

If you just BELIEVE that God sees you as right in His sight, the automatic effect begins to produce Holiness in your life without you even trying. That is the power of Grace!

Understand that the power of sin to control you has been destroyed. But it's now your choice to make. Will you give sin power over your life? Or will you choose to give God the rightful place as redeemer of your life?

It's Faith in Him through every circumstance that will conquer the forces that stand against you and strengthen you for the things you cannot change.

Simply pray and tell God –

"God, I can't clean myself and I don't have the strength to change anything. But I Believe in you and I Believe everything your word says about you. So here I am! Take me as I am and cleanse me and change me to be the man/woman you want me to be, and to have a life where you get all the glory!" Amen

# This Is Who We Are

It is easy to study fallen man and say this is who we are instead of studying Jesus and saying this is who we are.

**Colossians 1:21-23 (TPT)**

**Even though you were once distant from Him, living in the shadows of your evil thoughts and actions, He reconnected you back to Himself. He released His supernatural peace to you through the sacrifice of His own body as the sin-payment on your behalf so that you would dwell in His presence. And now there is nothing between you and Father God, for He sees you as holy, flawless, and restored, if indeed you continue to advance in faith, assured of a firm foundation to grow upon. Never be shaken from the hope of the gospel you have believed in. And this is the glorious news I preach all over the world.**

The truth is most of us have not heard about this HOPE Paul is speaking about in Colossians. We've probably all heard that we are sinners saved by God's Son because we were incapable and doomed to die in eternal damnation. Well that makes it seem that God felt so sorry for us that we were dead and dumb, that He had to be inconvenienced to come down here and save us all. If that were true, it takes a lot away from the value of our personal lives and the precious life of Jesus that He willingly puts inside of us.

The Bible says this about Jesus... 'For the joy set before Him He endured the cross.'

It says He now sees us as holy! He now sees us flawless and restored! The Bible says RECKON YOURSELVES dead to sin.

It teaches that HE BORE MY SIN in His body on the cross, so that we who have DIED TO SIN might live for RIGHTEOUSNESS!

It's important to understand what it means to "reckon" yourself dead to sin.

The definition of reckon is - to consider.

The definition of consider is - to regard.

The definition of regard is - to think of.

Think of yourself dead to sin.

Think of yourself dead to the memories of your sins.

Think of yourself dead to the stains of sin.

Think of yourself dead to the desire of sin.

From the understanding that we have died to sin because of Jesus, I submit to you that we can see His Life, and because of His sacrifice and atonement for our sins, we can say "THIS IS WHO WE ARE!

Day 9

**For He satisfies the thirsty and fills the hungry with Good Things - Psalm 107:9**

# The Empty Hour

## Matthew 25:1-13 (GNT)

### *The Parable of the Ten Young Women*

"At that time the Kingdom of heaven will be like this. Once there were ten young women who took their oil lamps and went out to meet the bridegroom. Five of them were foolish, and the other five were wise. The foolish ones took their lamps but did not take any extra oil with them, while the wise ones took containers full of oil for their lamps. The bridegroom was late in coming, so they began to nod and fall asleep.

"It was already midnight when the cry rang out, 'Here is the bridegroom! Come and meet him!' The ten young women woke up and trimmed their lamps. Then the foolish ones said to the wise ones, 'Let us have some of your oil, because our lamps are going out.' 'No, indeed,' the wise ones answered, 'there is not enough for you and for us. Go to the store and buy some for yourselves.'

So the foolish ones went off to buy some oil; and while they were gone, the bridegroom arrived. The five who were ready went in with him to the wedding feast, and

**the door was closed. "Later the others arrived. 'Sir, sir! Let us in!' they cried out. 'Certainly not, I don't know you,' the bridegroom answered."**

**And Jesus concluded, "Watch out, then, because you do not know the day or the hour.**

Growing up I remember hearing this story of the 10 Young Women - (or Virgins, or Bridesmaids) preached in church. Every time that the story was told it always ended with the preacher making a declaration of Jesus' return. It's almost like they wanted to place a 'Holy Fear' inside of the congregation, that if you were caught off guard when Jesus came back, He surely was going to lock you out because of your bad deeds. If you've ever heard the sermon preached on a Sunday morning, I'm sure that you've heard the same sort of closing behind the parable.

One day as I was reading through this story in Matthew - God gave me a different perspective.

I noticed that if the Kingdom in the story that Jesus told truly was a representation of God's Kingdom - then there was no importance of needing a certain amount of oil to be accepted into a Kingdom full of sufficiency.

And then the question changed... What if the reason the young women didn't get in wasn't the fact their lamps were empty? What if they didn't get in because they compared themselves to the other 5 Women, and left to go get something that they believed they needed, when the bridegroom had already paid the price to keep the entire Kingdom lit?

What if it was because they didn't know the covenant they were to become part of?

I propose to you - That JESUS IS ENOUGH and has done the work needed for everyone to be accepted. If your focus is on you and what you need to do or attain to make yourself acceptable in His sight, you might just run away before He shows up!

Don't believe the lie that there is something more that you need for the bridegroom to notice you.

The truth I see in this story is the fact that not only did the 5 young women count themselves as being in lack by comparison, but they also were nowhere to be found at the hour of His return!

I submit to you that the price Jesus paid for you is enough!

"BELIEF is always the way in, while UNBELIEF creates comparison and self-preservation which will ultimately lead you to perceive insufficiency in your life!"

# Under Oath

When we say we Believe in Jesus, it is important to know WHO we are saying we Believe in - and WHAT He did for us to Believe!

Let us never overlook the depth of His sacrifice. Let us never water it down to magical blessings, culture relevant messages, and pointing our fingers at plaques on the wall saying, "Jesus cares more about your doctrine than your soul!"

There is a 'Grace Walk' in our journey as believers, it begins with Faith and is ever growing in present Faith through every circumstance.

Remember this...

Just as truly as He came to die for you, He has come to live your life for you. When you trust Him as your dying Savior, you then earn the right and responsibility to trust Him as your living Savior.

"Just as much as He came to deliver you from future punishment - He also came to deliver you from present bondage." - Hannah Whitall Smith

He is with you today just as much as the day He rescued you!

# The Mind of Christ

To live in RIGHTEOUSNESS before God, means you can stand before God without guilt, shame, or condemnation.

Remember this - "The work of righteousness is any expression of God's nature through our lives."

## 2 Corinthians 5:21 (TPT)

**For God made the only one who did not know sin to become sin for us, so that we who did not know righteousness might become the righteousness of God through our union with him.**

The sin nature of man was cursed when Jesus who was without sin died on the cross. From that moment and through eternity a New Covenant was made with God, that through His Son, we no longer had to live a life with the sin nature mindset. We have been given the 'Mind of Christ', which is a mind in right standing with God!

I dare make the bold statement that because of Jesus; you have been given a life of PERFECTION! Not because you are perfect, but because HE IS PERFECT!

A mind that lives in this place will never give in to the power of sin over your life! It is a life obtained to live free from the identity, the stain, and the effects of sin.

If your heart is pure to live that way and even if you stumble into something, you will immediately run to God as a son and thank Him for righteousness and the washing of the blood. Grace isn't a free ride to sin and get away with it. It's the goodness of God that will lead a heart to repentance. And the desire of a true repentant heart will always want to live out the morality of God's will.

His Grace and Mercy separates you from the thing that causes you to stumble, and through communion with God you will be wiser, sharper, stronger and more complete than ever before! - Why?

Because it is the POWER OF RIGHTEOUSNESS! It is the MIND OF CHRIST!

# Times of Grace

"Grace is not the empowerment to stay the same; Grace is a guarantee to change."

Grace is God's power through HIS SON on OUR behalf to become LIKE HIM. Mercy is freely given by the heart of God to transform us and change us. His life is something that no one ever deserved.

When you receive God's mercy; it will draw you into the release of His beautiful grace, and thus you are saved by grace through faith! Through His grace you become more like Him as you yield to Him. His grace is like an edging tool, and a life in relationship with Him is like the picture in Isaiah 64 of the Potter molding the clay into perfection.

**Isaiah 64:8 (GNT) but you are our father, LORD. We are like clay, and you are like the potter. You created us...**

God wants to use the events we encounter each day as tools to shape and sculpt us into the image of Christ! His way of creating us into sons and daughters who look like Him isn't always easy, and it's not always the way we would choose. If we could change by our own strength and choice, then we wouldn't need Him. You can find rest and assurance by having faith and trusting that He is going to take care of you. This is His never wavering promise for your life.

Know this - "His process can take time, but Grace is always at work on your behalf. God will never leave you, and He'll never forsake you."

# **Believe**

We don't have to buy in to our salvation. Even if you had all the money in the world, there's no price tag on God's gift…

"There is no price to pay in order to purchase what He has already paid for."

The life of Jesus was not a bank loan or a credit card. There is no extra costs or extra fees taxed on the end when Jesus said, "It is finished".

All we must do is believe, receive, and freely give!

To BELIEVE means to -

BELIEVE in the One that He sent.

BELIEVE in the One who died for us.

BELIEVE in the One who came back to life so that we could have eternal life.

God loved you specifically before you even breathed oxygen to love anyone else, and He's empowered you with the same Spirit of Jesus that healed the sick, cast out demons, and raised the dead!

Know this - "It costs you nothing because it cost Him everything. Be confident in believing in Him! You were created for a purpose! And because of His Life given for you, you have been chosen, you have been redeemed, and you now have been given the same Spirit to tell the world just how good He really is!

Day 15

**Christianity is about being transformed into the likeness and image of Jesus. It's not just about asking Jesus for things we like.**

# Undivided

Jesus paid a valuable price to restore us from our separation and reunite us back to the Father. The beauty and power of His perfect plan and sacrifice is truly unimaginable!

It is in perfect union relationship with Holy Ghost where continual grace is released that enables us to walk out what His truth calls us to. By Grace we are saved, but it's through faith that we abide and rest in the finished work. For as we grow in God much is expected and required of us.

I used to think that Heaven was somewhere up in space and that I needed to draw near to God so that He would draw near to me. If you search around, it wouldn't be hard to find a collection of turn or burn teachings on holiness that use scriptures from the Bible like James 4:8 that says,

**James 4:8 (NKJV) Draw near to God and He will draw near to you. Cleanse your hands, you sinners; and purify your hearts, you double-minded.**

Most often the ones who teach this way are looked up to as being 'God's anointed vessels.' It turns into a position of the holy man pointing his finger at an unholy man. This is an example of religious legalism and can be misleading for some. Many people have been left with feelings of inadequacy because of the lack of love in communicating the Gospel. I also felt this way for many years of my life. I thought a lifestyle of Christianity was scary, boring, and way too hard.

But there is something about when James was writing that I want to point out. James was speaking to a Jewish crowd that had grown up their entire lives following the laws of Moses. It is important to understand history and the cultural timelines when we read the scriptures. For example, these Jews did believe that one day the Messiah was going to come and deliver them, but at that time, they were still uncertain if Jesus really was who He said He was. James calls them 'double-minded'. And he says "sinners", because before you are born again and have accepted Christ as savior, you are still bound by the sin of the garden, and you are by default a sinner.

But there is good news! You and I who have received the gift of Salvation are no longer divided!

God is not in some invisible realm up in the sky. You don't have to kick, cry, and scream to get His attention.

Because you have received Him, you are now one with Him and you are truly undivided!

**Galatians 3:26-28 (NKJV) for you are all sons of God through faith in Christ Jesus. For as many of you as were baptized into Christ have put on Christ. There is neither Jew nor Greek, there is neither slave nor free, there is neither male nor female; for you are all one in Christ Jesus.**

# The Fable of Good or Bad

Once there was a farmer whose horse ran away. His neighbor came over to tell him he felt sorry for him, only to be told in return: "Who knows what is good or bad?"

The next day the horse returned, bringing with it eleven wild horses it had met during its adventurous escape. The neighbor came over again, this time to congratulate the farmer on his good fortune. Only to be told once again "Who knows what is good or bad?"

The next day the farmer's son tried to tame one of the wild horses and fell off, breaking his leg. His neighbor came back again one more time to express how bad he felt, but for the third time all the farmer said was: "Who knows what is good or bad?"

And once again the farmer was correct, for this time, the king of that land had started a war and the following day soldiers came by to draft all young men into the army, but because of his injury the son was not taken.

There is a point to make in this famous Chinese fable of good and bad. We cannot always see or know why things happen.

Only God knows every reason and we can't put our own understanding before His doing.

It's not fair to say we love and trust Him, then live with questionable doubt that takes away our love and replaces it with fear.

Love is a choice. It's not an involuntary action. God spoke love and free will into the very being of our existence. His goal is not to take away your freedom. His desire is to draw you into His goodness by giving you the ability to make choices.

It is often hard to endure and understand the challenges we go through in life. But it's important that as we grow in spiritual maturity, we learn to not give in to the stress and worry.

I assure you everything happens for a reason... God has a reason.

Even when you don't understand or don't have things figured out; Trust in Him and know that it will all come into alignment in His perfect timing.

# Rise Within

Sometimes it can feel like everything is shaking all around you. And it's ok to admit that you find it hard to believe when you feel like you're being tested.

I want you to know that it's not God's will that we all have to live through a horrible experience in our lives. And He's not some cruel and twisted God that enjoys watching His children go through pain and punishment.

Know this – There is always something to be learned in the testing moments of our lives. Even in the most trying difficulties, He still uses every situation for His Glory.

"There is precious gold inside of you that is yet to be discovered."

Just as gold is found in the earth, it is also buried in you. The Lord uses these moments that shake us just like shaking a gold pan in a river amid overflowing waters.

These times of shaking cause the gold in you to rise to the surface and if the pan is shaken hard enough, eventually, gold will be the only thing remaining.

Then, the gold inside of you is put through the fire to remove the impurities.

When the heat is turned up high enough, the gold will rise to the occasion and be revealed apart from the dross.

Once you are shaken long enough, FAITH WILL RISE, ENDURANCE WILL COME, and ETERNAL FRUIT WILL GROW!

These trials which are not always joyful moments are for a much better you than you think.

They cause you to make a choice.

They force you to confront what you really believe in your heart.

Do you really trust in God? - Do you believe God will surely come and destroy the devourer? - Do you believe He will surely make the crooked paths straight?

Look at the current circumstances in your life and ask yourself, would you have faith without the testing? And who would you be right now without the suffering?

"Consider these times as opportunities for great joy!"

**James 1:2-4 (NLT)**

**Dear brothers and sisters, when troubles of any kind come your way, consider it an opportunity for great joy. For you know that when your faith is tested, your endurance has a chance to grow. So let it grow, for when your endurance is fully developed, you will be perfect and complete, needing nothing.**

# Divine Nature

**2 Peter 1:2-4 (NLT) May God give you more and more grace and peace as you grow in your knowledge of God and Jesus our Lord.**

By his divine power, God has given us everything we need for living a godly life. We have received all of this by coming to know him, the one who called us to himself by means of his marvelous glory and excellence. And because of his glory and excellence, he has given us great and precious promises. These are the promises that enable you to share his divine nature and escape the world's corruption caused by human desires.

It's through God's word and truth that we gain an understanding of our identity as sons and daughters, and it's how we can begin to recognize the divine nature of Christ. We are to live a lifestyle every day to honor Jesus, because He gave His life for us to live. The enemy wants you to question who you are, because he knows he cannot shake God off the throne. He can't change God's mind about you; therefore, he does his very best to change your mind about God.

This statement has been proven time and time again since the beginning of creation! The devil wants you to question what God has said about you, and the answer to that question is simple…

"You are worthy of God's love because God said so. You are redeemed because the cross said so. And you have the Holy Spirit because the Son was willing to give His life for you!"

When we learn to walk in righteousness and without fear, we will be able to produce extraordinary accomplishments, not because of WHO WE ARE but because of WHO HE IS!

Day 20

**"The difference between living in forgiveness and living in righteousness is that when you look into the mirror every day and you are living in righteousness; you no longer see someone who sins, but you see the one who paid the price for you to live free from sin!"**

# The Torn Veil

God longs to encounter you.

He wants your heart's affection every day.

He longs for a relationship with you.

He knew humanity would never be able to dethrone our self-preservation and ambitions as a sacrifice. So, HE HIMSELF came down from His throne to become a sacrifice for US!

We were once separated from His holiness.

We were once separated from His perfection.

But we were bought with the precious blood of Jesus; the sacrifice of God's chosen lamb!

When the veil was torn, God came for you. Heaven paid a high price so that you could return to Him as a son or as a daughter. There is no longer a separation from Him.

By exchanging your life for His, He washes your sins away. He changes you from the inside out. He mends your hurts and takes away the pain of the world. His love is complete, and it fills the void inside of you. His love is relentless, and it pursues you beyond all the chaos, the darkness, and the oppression.

"I believe that when Jesus who was perfect in every way, hung on the cross, you were on His mind. And it was your life that He thought was of such worth to be paid for by His Holy Love!"

# **<u>Words of Hope</u>**

The LORD will fight for you; you need only to be still.

"You do not realize now what I am doing, but later you will understand."

So do not fear, for I am with you; do not be dismayed, for I am your God.

I will strengthen you and help you; I will uphold you with my righteous right hand.

Be strong and courageous. Do not be afraid or terrified because of them, for the LORD your God goes with you; he will never leave you nor forsake you.

For I know the plans I have for you," declares the LORD, "plans to prosper you and not to harm you, plans to give you hope and a future.

"Come to me, all you who are weary and burdened, and I will give you rest. Take my yoke upon you and learn from me, for I am gentle and humble in heart, and you will find rest for your souls. For my yoke is easy and my burden is light."

Those who hope in the LORD will renew their strength. They will soar on wings like eagles; they will run and not grow weary; they will walk and not be faint.

Be confident of this, that he who began a good work in you will carry it on to completion until the day of Christ Jesus.

**Exodus 14:14, John 13:7, Isaiah 41:10, Deuteronomy 31:6, Jeremiah 29:11**

**Matthew 11:28-30, Isaiah 40:31, Philippians 1:6**

# Paid in Full

One afternoon, a priority mail package was delivered to my home. As I noticed the delivery box sitting on my front doorstep, I suddenly heard the words,

"WHAT FAITH YOU PUT IN HUMANITY."

I saw a clear picture of how often we put faith into people with online shopping, mail orders, and online deliveries. If the logistics say that we will receive our ordered product on a certain day, we put trust in people and technology to follow through.

Another example is the workplace payday, so often we place trust in financial institutions and deposits. We make plans in our lives based on someone else's decision to follow through.

It's incredible the amount of faith we have placed in humanity, even in manmade computer systems to keep up with money and lifestyles.

Yet for the CREATOR of ALL things…

The ONE who GAVE us the very air we breathe…

The ONE who ALLOWED us to be born and wake up today…

And the ONE who HOLDS all things in his hands…

We have such a HARD time believing in our breakthrough, because it's not visible.

After Bible College, I worked full-time in the mail room at Daystar Network Television in Texas. I've seen every step of distribution from the ordering process to package handling and delivery.

If you look at every detail that goes into these types of online orders, you will be introduced to a lot of unseen yet vital and important steps. (How and when the order was selected, packaged, quantity, stamped, loaded, shipped, etc.)

I believe it is safe to say that even more vital and important steps are involved when it comes to our lives, including our prayers and answers. I hope this brings to light a revelation that you will never forget.

It's in God's perfect plan that we don't see how it's going to happen, because we couldn't contain the details and the scale of administration during the supernatural battles around us.

"It's an HONOR and BLESSING that Jesus has gone before us and that He made a way possible.

Often in the middle of the most difficult trials we face, it's hard to remember the fact that God has already achieved the VICTORY. When we keep our eyes fixed on the problems, we lose focus of the promise.

I remind you - Jesus has already won! He conquered the grave and He restored your life back to righteousness!

Believe that He is with you and believe He knows what's best for you. He knows every detail of your life!

Take a moment and pray – "God, I thank you for loving me. Thank you for giving me life. I thank you for the cross, and for restoration through your sacrifice for me. I believe in you. And I believe that the current process of my life is in your hands. Thank you for going before me and thank you for the victory over this life's circumstances. I put my trust in you because I believe that the price of my life was paid in full! And I give honor to you!"

"In your holy name... amen."

# Deep Waters

**Isaiah 43:2 (NLT) "When you go through deep waters I will be with you. When you go through rivers of difficulty, you will not drown. When you walk through the fire of oppression, you will not be burned up; the flames will not consume you."**

I propose to you this revelation - "Love is complete only when there is an opposing force challenging it."

God's grace over you is MORE THAN ENOUGH to erase all your sins and your past completely!

He has plans for your life even if you don't know what that looks like.

You are NOT a mistake, and you WERE NOT born just to suffer and die! If you've ever felt in your heart that there is more to live for, you're right!

Be encouraged today that Jesus loves you and He paid the ultimate price and died for you, so that you can have a life worth living for!

There is a whole world of God's goodness and peace available just for you! And it starts with saying YES and BELIEVING in Jesus!

HE is peace! - HE will make you whole! - HE will deliver you! - HE will keep you from the fires! - And HE will set your feet on solid ground!

Day 25

**I'm absolutely convinced that nothing—nothing living or dead, angelic or demonic, today or tomorrow, high or low, thinkable or unthinkable—absolutely nothing can get between us and God's love because of the way that Jesus our Master has embraced us.**

**- Romans 8:38-39 (MSG)**

# We Are One

The purpose of Jesus giving His life for us goes beyond a finishing act that enables us to enter Heaven one day. His sacrifice cleansed us, so that we could be reunited with the Father, and His Spirit clothes us in His Righteousness. We gained an inheritance of sonship through the cross. The problem most people have in believing this is that they fully don't understand who He is in us, and who we are in Him.

"Our closeness with God is not a feeling, it's a fact."

**1 Corinthians 15:22 (NKJV) - as in Adam all die, even so in Christ all shall be made alive.**

**Colossians 1:27 (NLT) - and this is the secret: Christ lives in you. This gives you assurance of sharing his glory.**

**1 Corinthians 6:17 (NIV) - but whoever is united with the Lord is one with him in spirit**

Notice what the three passages of scripture are saying to us...

1 Corinthians 15 says, "in Christ."

Colossians 1 says, "Christ lives in you."

1 Corinthians 6 says, "One with Him in spirit."

In the early years of my salvation, my prayers were that God would 'draw near to me every day' and that I wanted 'less of me and more of Him.' I honestly thought this was how I was supposed to pray. For my lack of knowledge, it felt like God was far away in a perfect, unreachable realm. I felt like God was a 'giant force' and my best hope was that He would comply to my requests. I thought the prayers that pleased Him needed to be a plea for Him to come down into my life and fix my mess occasionally. This approach to what I thought was a relationship with Him seemed right. Dare I say that some of you reading this now may still be living with the same kind of approach to prayer like I did, and if so, I have good news...

God gave His Son so that we did not have to live a life in separation from Him.

Before Jesus went to the cross, He prayed for you and me... and this was that prayer -

**John 17:21 (NLT)**

**I pray that they will all be one, just as you and I are one—as you are in me, Father, and I am in you. And may they be in us so that the world will believe you sent me.**

Jesus prayed that we would be one with Him! And the moment He gave His life for us, that prayer was answered! God answered His Son's prayers!

We truly must see the reflection of Him in our hearts. Every secular attire and worldly view of religious works will always weigh down like a rock tied to your leg. God doesn't want you to live a fake or pretend perfect life. He knows we sometimes fail or can even sometimes struggle.

It's through the identity of the Son Jesus Christ that we become who God has called us to be.

We as believers must understand what we have been given through Jesus in order to live a Christ-like life. There is no rule book, or strategy guide, or 12 step program that will ever work apart from His Holy Spirit.

Believing in Christ, trusting in the finished work, and living each day in Him is the only way that you will ever find His perfect will, pure and fulfilling satisfaction, and true undeniable rest in your life.

Day 27

# **The Tempter**

In Roman history, when a person was convicted of a crime punishable by death and condemned to die by crucifixion, they were tied to the crossbar of the cross. They would carry it from the point of their conviction to the place where they would die an agonizing and brutal death.

We see this in the story of Jesus who had to carry His cross through the streets of Jerusalem to Golgotha so that the He could take the punishment of our sins.

The happening of the cross and agonizing torture of Jesus, was so that your condemnation is carried to the place of Christ's death, and it doesn't go any further. All your past failures, your present failures, and even your future mistakes were laid down the moment that Jesus gave up His life for you. Your sin was forgiven.

Every attempt of the enemy to bring you down by condemnation has already been handled by conviction of your failures and the ruling of the death of Jesus for your sins. There is no new attack of Satan. It's been the same since the Garden of Eden.

The only difference in the attack, is the form of the question and who it comes from…. "Did God Say?"

In Matthew 4:1-11, the devil came to tempt Jesus. Jesus replied to the same question with this answer,

## Matthew 4:4 (NKJV)

**... "Man shall not live by bread alone but by every word that proceeds from the mouth of God!"**

If Jesus didn't fall for Satan's attempt that day in the desert, there is no way that He would fall for the attempt today. You are IN CHRIST, and He is IN YOU! And because He has given you the authority of His Holy Spirit, you don't have to give in to the lies of the enemy either!

Your journey can be filled with moments of uncertainty, but rest assured, that every word of God still stands. Every promise - Every prophecy- Every decree over who you are and what you've been called to is still the same as it was the day that He died for you!

The question "Did God Say?" is not even a question!

You are His and you are loved!

WE LIVE BY FAITH!"

# **Perfect Union**

There is great potential to do greater things for God, but many times our eyesight is limited, and we only see the problem not the solution.

It's more about walking in God's unlimited presence and less about walking with man's limited principles.

When we look at Christianity through a clouded and hardened religious lens, we will see that we gave our life to Jesus and now it's up to us to follow God's law to make sure that we stay saved. And if we miss it, we better 'repent' and dwell in that place of condemnation, because God will have nothing to do with us if we don't live the rest of our lives feeling bad about what we've done. If this were true, then the accountability of works and doing right would wear us down so bad, that are failed intentions would eventually disqualify us.

It took me years to understand that it's not about our works and struggling with condemning faults. I remember times of feeling that something I had done caused the Lord to be disappointed in me. It made me feel like the only way to make Him happy again was to lock myself in a room and stay away from everything worldly that I possibly could. Somehow there grew the notion that once we're saved, we must be careful and don't get close to the bad people that aren't saved. And hopefully God will come and rescue us before the world destroys itself, because His goal was to unleash wrath and destroy it one day anyway! It sounds crazy, but unfortunately, I have met a lot of people who believed this way.

The born-again life of a believer is not to get free from the bondage of sin and fall into the bondage of religion. As a matter of fact, it's about walking in freedom, walking empowered by the Spirit of Christ, walking as a light in the darkness, and going about doing good JUST LIKE CHRIST DID!

The definition of repent is to feel or express sincere regret about wrongdoing. It includes a sense of sorrow and the morality of doing the right thing. In Christianity, repentance takes the role in redirecting a man or women to a continual posture of their heart. It is often defined as an action or turning away from self-serving activities and turning to God, to walk in His ways.

"True Repentance leads to a transformation that takes place in the believer. It changes our old ways of thinking by the renewing of the mind to God's way of thinking."

My entire life I never heard anyone say that Jesus gave His life to me. I only understood that He gave His

life for me. Many people are unaware of this language because it's usually not what the preacher says to get you to receive salvation at the end of a Sunday morning church service.

The statement I am about to make is what I had never been told, and it is what changed my life forever...

Jesus gives His life to you, and through the authority of His Spirit in you, you can change or 'repent' from the way that you see things. This is what it means to be empowered by the Spirit of Christ!

God knew that we had no power over sin and the lies of the enemy. He watched Adam and Eve who were created in His very own image fall into the attack of unbelief. If we look at ourselves apart from God, then we'll see ourselves as weak and unable to continue the journey that we are on. But if we see ourselves in perfect union with Him, we will find HIS STRENGTH in our weakness to be more than enough to overcome.

If we walk into a lion's den as a sheep dressed in a lion's coat, we'll eventually be sniffed out and caught, but if we carry the whip, we will take control.

I like to say it this way - "If we play with fire we will eventually get burned!

But if we become the fire, everything around us will be set ablaze!"

# The Father's Heart

My understanding of God the Father and His love for me as a son has been a growth process for many years of my life. I grew up in church and was taught scriptures and the do's/don'ts, but I was never taught the 'Father's heart'.

You see now that I'm much older and have my own kids, I can see a side of love that I never knew before. From the things that I learned, I always felt like I needed to work hard to please God. I felt like the more that I could produce for Him, the more pleased He would be in me. If this were true however, in John 3:16 that reads, "for God so loved the world that he gave his only son" would've been written much different. It would have read, "if you are able to be good enough, God will love you enough to send His only son."

"It's not the production of my works that determines the value of my life. It's How much He loves us that determines the life we have been given."

Years ago, I was planting a garden in front of our home in East Texas. My youngest son who was then 5 years old was outside with me. He insisted that he was working with me. Although he was there, and I was enjoying him being there, he was hardly doing any helping of the sort. The yard tools were too sharp, and the bags of soil were too heavy for him to move. He still in his little innocent mind thought that he was helping.

was a priceless moment to see his little heart burn to do what I was doing and with great intention. In that moment, I began to see myself through God's eyes.

When my 5-year-old son went to lift a 40-pound bag of soil, he couldn't even nudge it, yet still with a look of intent he kept grunting and pulling up on the corners to try and lift it. I leaned down and grabbed one end of the bag and began to drag it. He got behind it and pushed. His heart was filled with excitement to be helping dad. My heart was filled with excitement because I loved him.

Through the years I've noticed many different times where my son has been eager to help me. For example, setting the dishes before we eat a meal together, or throwing the trash when he sees me already in the process of doing it. Almost every time, I allow him to jump in and take over each task. It's not because I need him to. Honestly, I'm perfectly capable of doing these things on my own, but there is something special about these moments when a father's heart is full. The love that I have and the connection between my son and I are intensified when moments like this occur.

Truthfully, there is nothing that he could ever do or not do to make me love him any less.

This realization has given me hope, as it should you. You see, God doesn't need us to do 'His work'. The creator of the universe is perfectly capable of taking care of you and me.

"Trusting in Him and relying on Him are the greatest challenges that anyone can face."

We know of His goodness, and we know He is way bigger than we are, yet we can somehow still find ourselves striving to do what we think needs to be done for the completion our lives to fall into place.

But He doesn't require you to do this life alone or to pay a price that He's already paid for you. He doesn't want you to go through life worrying and battling the way you think things should be. Honestly, almost anything that is set before you will be too big for you to handle alone if it's truly something He has given you. The truth is He loves you too much to see you hurt or feeling broken with missing pieces.

Remember this - "His joy is a love that isn't created by what you do or don't do for him. He simply loves you because you are His. He allows each of us to sit at his table. He welcomes us all home, and He clothes each of us in His finest robes of righteousness. It's only for His namesake that we can partake in the goodness of that very same love He has for us."

I have learned that all the prophetic words, all the teachings, all the prayers, all the songs, all the stages, all the miracles, and all the callings of our lives are From Him - Through Him - and For Him! It's all His! And it's only in TRUSTING our Father, BELIEVING that we are His, and HAVING FAITH that HE is in control that we could even come close to the same love that He has for us.

Day 30

**"The highest reward that you will ever receive for the things that you have been through is not what you gain from it, but what you become by it."**

# The Good News

For years I've shared my testimony to bring people face to face with the salvation of Jesus Christ. I've seen hundreds give their lives in repentance. I've seen countless powerful miracles.

Even after all the wonderful signs that point to Him, I'm still amazed at how little we know of the truth of why Jesus gave his life for us.

If I asked you what is your definition of the Gospel? What would be your response?

Yes, Jesus came to give us eternal life and yes, He came to forgive our sins...

But what if I told you there was more?

This book is a collection of short writings from my personal journey of Faith. It was written from the thankfulness of my salvation, not by someone who pretends to live a self-righteous fantasy of being perfect.

I've struggled again and again in my own unbelief and wasted a lot of years trying to find success in my own selfish ways of doing things.

I was stuck in the deception of religion for a long time. It birthed in me a negative understanding of the church. Religious condemnation attached itself to my mind.

It was judgmental and weary. The challenges kept me in a place of failure and feeling defeated.

After what seemed to feel like 35 years of darkness, a holy fire of truth pierced deep into my heart. It was by the revelation power of the Holy Spirit, and through God's Word, that I finally found freedom. Rightly dividing the Word and the simple truths of the Gospel allowed me for the first time to understand what I had signed up for the day I said 'yes' to Jesus. That fire and love burned down every stronghold of deception in me, and I finally knew what it meant to be born again.

This is what I call... The Beautiful Change.

This book was written to help the reader understand the truths of identity in Christ and help jumpstart the renewing of their mind. I prayed that it would equip Christians to better share the Gospel, and that it would empower them with a deeper understanding and intimacy of God's goodness.

But...

The purpose of this book would not be fulfilled without a proper invitation to the greatest moment of your life.

Your own personal Beautiful Change!

The Bible tells us that in the beginning God created everything. He created the heavens and the earth and everything in it. He created humans and gave them free will, but along with free will, He gave them one rule. That rule was to obey Him.

They broke that rule by disobeying God, and because of their disobedience sin came into the world. The world became a broken and fallen place filled with sickness, death, wars, and plagues. It was no longer the perfect world that God had created.

From the beginning God had a plan. His plan was to one day restore all things and make all things new again. He would bring things back to perfection, but before He would do that, He had to deal with root cause of all the problems. The problem was sin. The Bible tells us, the punishment for sin is death, and because God is merciful, He sent His only begotten Son Jesus Christ to pay the price on our behalf.

Jesus was born of a virgin and of the Holy Spirit. He lived a perfect sinless life. And while Jesus was here on this earth He preached the message of God, to REPENT and BELIEVE for the kingdom of heaven is at hand.

The deceived religious people hated Him, and they did not receive His message. They wanted to silence Him, so they devised a plan to have Him crucified on a cross. Jesus willingly gave up His life and died an agonizing and horrible death. His innocent blood was shed as the judgement for the sins of the world.

Jesus was buried in a tomb, but on the third day, He came back to life! He conquered sin and death forever! Jesus is now sitting at the right hand of His Father (God). He has been crowned in glory, and all authority has been given to Him. And one day He is coming back to restore all things and make them brand new again.

Jesus told His disciples and every believer to prepare for His return. He said that we would not know when He is coming, so we must always be ready.

To prepare for His return we must -

1. Repent - to turn from your sinful ways and turn to God's ways.

2. Declare that Jesus is Lord and believe He was raised from the dead.

3. Be baptized in water (full- immersion) for the remission of your sins.

4. Be filled with the Holy Spirit. The Holy Spirit will help you, lead you, and prepare you for Jesus' return.

This is a prayer of REPENTANCE and RECIEVING the Salvation of Jesus.

*Jesus, I know that according to Your Word in John 3:3, I must be born again to see the kingdom of God. I know I am a sinner. I believe you died for me. I believe that you shed your blood on the cross for me. And I believe on the third day you rose again from the dead.*

*I repent and turn from my sins. Holy Spirit, I need you.*

*I no longer want to be in control of my life. Please make your home in me. Forgive me of my sins and be my Lord and Savior from this day forward.*

*I receive your strength and power by your precious Holy Spirit.*

*I turn to you, and I want to live for you.*

*Jesus, thank you for the gift of salvation... I promise to forever obey you with the help of Holy Spirit and to follow you all the days of my life. In Jesus' Name. Amen*

Congratulations!

If you prayed this prayer in all sincerity, you are now a Child of God and have turned from your old way of living. However, it is very important that you follow through with water baptism and the filling of the Holy Spirit.

I encourage you to connect with a local church in your city. If you don't have a local church, I invite you to email my contact address (at the end of this book).

Be encouraged to tell someone else about your new faith in Christ, and more importantly, spend time with God each day through prayer and Bible reading.

Thank you for reading this book!

Let us know about the decision you made and how this book has impacted you! We are rejoicing with you!

**Armando Perez**

**Contact : aperezbooks@outlook.com**

My prayer over you is - **Ephesians 1:16-23 (NLT)**

I have not stopped thanking God for you. I pray for you constantly, asking God, the glorious Father of our Lord Jesus Christ, to give you spiritual wisdom and insight so that you might grow in your knowledge of God. I pray that your hearts will be flooded with light so that you can understand the confident hope he has given to those he called—his holy people who are his rich and glorious inheritance.

I also pray that you will understand the incredible greatness of God's power for us who believe him. This is the same mighty power that raised Christ from the dead and seated him in the place of honor at God's right hand in the heavenly realms.

Now he is far above any ruler or authority or power or leader or anything else—not only in this world but also in the world to come. God has put all things under the authority of Christ and has made him head over all things for the benefit of the church. And the church is his body; it is made full and complete by Christ, who fills all things everywhere with himself.